The SPORTS HEROES Library

Basketball's PLAYMAKERS

Nathan Aaseng

 Lerner Publications Company • Minneapolis

ACKNOWLEDGMENTS: The photographs are reproduced through the courtesy of: pp. 4, 18, 20, 26, 46, Wide World Photos, Inc.; pp. 8, 13, 64, 68, 70, Los Angeles Lakers; p. 11, Michigan State University; p. 16, Photography, Inc.; pp. 23, 25, 44, 45, Boston Celtics; pp. 28, 31, 33, 34, Detroit Pistons; pp. 35, 54, Washington Bullets, Gary Fine; p. 39, Indiana University; pp. 42, 72, 80, Milwaukee Bucks; p. 50, Portland Trailblazers; p. 53, Indiana Pacers (Steve Snoddy, Tracfoto); p. 58, Houston Rockets; p. 60, Golden State Warriors; p. 67, Duquesne University; pp. 76, 78, 79, Kansas City Kings. Cover photograph by John E. Biever.

To the staff at the St. Louis Park library branch

LIBRARY OF CONGRESS CATALOGING IN PUBLICATION DATA

Aaseng, Nathan.
Basketball's playmakers.

(The Sports heroes library)
Summary: Biographies of eight basketball players noted for their talent in calling plays and setting up shots. Included are Earvin "Magic" Johnson, Nate "Tiny" Archibald, Kevin Porter, Quinn Buckner, Johnny Davis, John Lucas, Norm Nixon, and Phil Ford.
  1. Guards (Basketball) — United States — Biography — Juvenile literature. 2. Basketball — United States — Juvenile literature. [1. Basketball players] I. Title. II. Series.
GV884.A1A24   1983   796.32′3′0922 [B] [920]   83-1041
ISBN 0-8225-1330-7 (lib. bdg.)

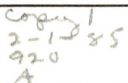

Copyright © 1983 by Lerner Publications Company

All rights reserved. International copyright secured. No part of this book may be reproduced in any form whatsoever without permission in writing from the publisher except for the inclusion of brief quotations in an acknowledged review.
Manufactured in the United States of America
International Standard Book Number: 0-8225-1330-7
Library of Congress Catalog Card Number: 83-1041

1 2 3 4 5 6 7 8 9 10 92 91 90 89 88 87 86 85 84 83

Contents

	Introduction	5
1	Earvin "Magic" Johnson	9
2	Nate "Tiny" Archibald	19
3	Kevin Porter	29
4	Quinn Buckner	37
5	Johnny Davis	47
6	John Lucas	55
7	Norm Nixon	63
8	Phil Ford	73

Magic Johnson (32) shares a rebound with teammate Kurt Rambis in the 1982 championship game against Philadelphia. In the series, Magic proved the value of a playmaker by winning his second Most Valuable Player honor in three years.

Introduction

There are a good many pro basketball guards who must be wondering what football quarterbacks have that they don't have. After all, these guards do the same jobs football quarterbacks do. They lead the offense, direct the players to their positions, call the plays, and handle the ball most of the time. They can open up the game to a freewheeling offensive flurry, or they can slow it down to a patient, conservative attack. It is their job to figure out what will work against a defense and to see that the ball gets to their high-scoring teammates.

Despite all of the similarities, a quarterback and a basketball playmaker stand on opposite ends of the glamour scale. Quarterbacks are the most famous stars in football, and they are protected from the punishment that most of their teammates take on each play. Basketball playmakers, however, are among the least famous in their sport. Far from being protected, they are asked to do many of the grubbiest jobs in the game. They must scramble around players setting up screens and try to defend against taller players who like to take them inside towards the basket. They are often seen charging into massive bodies near the basket in order to draw attention away from a hot-shooting teammate.

Unlike a quarterback, however, a playmaker does not dominate the offensive statistics. His performance, in fact, is likely to be buried underneath the shooting statistics of his high-scoring teammates. Most box scores in the newspapers print only shooting and rebounding numbers, with no mention of playmaking statistics such as assists or turnovers.

Actually, the playmaker does not even have an official title. His position is simply listed as "guard," although coaches use a wide variety of terms to describe his role: playmaker, floor leader, floor general, point guard, ball-handler, etc.

While these playmakers are sometimes ignored by the fans, they are constantly in demand with coaches. That is because there is no point in having good shooters if no one can get the ball to them.

Besides doing the obvious things, such as bringing the ball downcourt and setting up plays, the playmaker has a special value to a team. Although there are no statistics to measure it, the playmaker is responsible for making the action happen. It is difficult in pro ball to find an open shot near the basket. The defenses have improved to the point where few players are able to work themselves open for a good shot. The playmaker can help by penetrating close to the basket and drawing defenders toward him. This usually leaves a teammate open for a shot.

A few flashy passers such as Magic Johnson have made a name for themselves in pro basketball. But it remains a fact that the playmakers have done their job the best when others have gotten the credit for the scoring. Like a movie director who is never seen by the public, the eight men in this book quietly run the show in pro basketball.

Guarded by Kansas City's Reggie King, Magic directs a Laker fast break.

1
Earvin "Magic" Johnson

For centuries it has been said that one little smile can brighten a person's day. But until recently, no one would have guessed that a smile also had the power to help win a National Basketball Association (NBA) title. Of course, Magic Johnson has brought more than a healthy set of teeth to the Los Angeles Lakers. He is a player of so many skills that, in a time of specialized roles in basketball, Johnson can and has played every position on the court. But his trademark has been the smile and enthusiasm that have charged up the veteran Lakers as nothing else had been able to do. Few floor leaders have ever done as fine a job at sparking their teammates to a top level of play.

Earvin Johnson was born in Lansing, Michigan, in

1959. He was one of 10 children whom his parents worked to support—his mother in the school system and his father for the auto industry. Earvin figured that his parents deserved their rest on weekends, so one Sunday morning he went out to play basketball without bothering to tell them. When his parents found out that he had left the house unannounced, they were upset and told him not to go out ever again without leaving word. From that time on, their son woke them up early every morning, as regularly as an alarm clock, to say he was on his way to the basketball court.

Johnson thought it would be an honor to see his name in the newspaper, so in high school he set himself the goal of making All-City to be certain to make the sports page at least once. He so far overshot his goal that it was like a bunter hoping to place a sacrifice bunt and ending up with a home run. Johnson earned the nickname "Magic" for his passing displays and was a regular entry in the local paper. After leading his team to the state title, he found recruiters from colleges flocking after him.

Magic always had a soft spot for underdogs so in 1977 he chose to attend Michigan State University rather than a stronger basketball school. In his freshman season, he helped pull the Spartans, who

During Magic's two seasons at Michigan State, the Spartans improved from a losing team to Big Ten Conference and then national champions.

had finished 10-17 the year before, to the Big Ten Conference championship.

Johnson did not score or rebound that much and averaged about 17 points and 8 rebounds per game. The average fan looking at a Michigan State box score must have wondered why everyone was raving about this new player. But Magic's leadership, graceful passes, and the way he could shred a defense had to be seen to be appreciated. During

11

his sophomore year, college fans across the country had a chance to see him in action when he led the Spartans to the national collegiate finals. There he outplayed Indiana State's star, Larry Bird, and was voted the tournament's Most Valuable Player for leading his team to a 75-64 win.

Although Johnson could have played two more years in college, in 1979 he sought the challenges of playing in the pros. The Los Angeles Lakers needed a colorful star who could bring fans into the arena. They believed Johnson would fill their needs, so they drafted the youngster in the first round. A number of scouts, however, thought Magic had a bigger reputation than he deserved. According to their reports, he was only an average shooter and an ordinary jumper and was slow on defense. All of this spelled trouble for Johnson, who also did not fit the job description of any pro position. At almost 6 feet, 9 inches, he was taller than any guard in pro history. But because of his leadership skills, the Lakers tried Magic at that spot.

From the first practice, Magic showed that he knew how the game should be played. He directed the offense like a veteran and was not afraid to wave players 10 years older than he into position. He controlled the ball on fast breaks, and his sharp

Earvin "Magic" Johnson

passes kept his teammates especially alert. None of them wanted to be embarrassed by getting hit in the chest with an unexpected pass! Instead of waiting around for someone to get open on offense, Johnson and his mates made their own openings with their running and quick passes. It was a special bonus to the Lakers when Magic proved he could shoot and rebound better in the pros than he had in college.

Even more important than all of these contributions, though, was the way that Magic made the game fun. At first some of the Lakers were nearly knocked over by Johnson's joyful hugs. His clapping and cheering reminded them of a high school pep rally. But the cool, businesslike pros who ordinarily sneered at the "rah rah" college approach found they could not resist Magic's warmth and enthusiasm. It began to rub off on them, and players such as Kareem Abdul-Jabbar seemed years younger as they flew around the court.

In the spring of 1980, the Lakers made the playoffs and faced the defending champions, the Seattle Supersonics. They had trouble matching the Sonics' muscle and lost the first game, 108-107. Lonnie Shelton, a rugged 6-foot, 8-inch, 245-pound forward, gave the Laker forwards a rough time in the battle for rebounds, so Los Angeles turned to Johnson to do something about it. Suddenly the playmaking guard became a power forward, and his surprising strength on the boards helped the Lakers sweep the final four games to win the series.

In the finals against Philadelphia, the Lakers closed steadily towards a championship. Jabbar was in top form as he led the Lakers to a 3-2 lead in games. In the fifth game, however, he sprained his ankle and was forced out of action. Without the 33 points and 13 rebounds that Jabbar had averaged in the series, the Lakers seemed to be no match for the 76ers. In a desperate move, they asked Johnson to fill in at center.

The position of center was completely new to Magic, but he refused to be terrified by the challenge. Like a small child, he could hardly contain his excitement and insisted on sitting in Jabbar's usual seat on the airplane flight. As he went out for the center jump against 7-foot Caldwell Jones, he chuckled to himself at the thought of a guard playing center in a championship game.

Surprisingly, Magic was not swept away by the huge 76er front line. The Lakers battled from eight points back to tie the score at halftime, 60-60. By then Magic was starting to enjoy his new role. Having a ball-handling guard playing close to the basket was like setting up spy headquarters in the middle of an enemy camp. Johnson passed, dribbled, and scored on his large opponents and astounded them by worming his way in for rebounds.

With five minutes to play, the Lakers had matched the 76ers point for point. Then Johnson completely took over. He scored on a tap-in and added nine points in the final 2½ minutes to seal the win.

With Johnson playing at center, the experts had expected a total mismatch at that position. They were right, only it was Magic who had rolled over

Even on defense, Johnson's flashy style delighted fans, as shown here in the 1980 championship finals against the 76ers.

his opponents. He had scored 42 points and grabbed 15 rebounds to win the series' Most Valuable Player Award.

The next season, Magic returned to his familiar spot at guard but suffered an injury early in the year. When he finally returned to the lineup in Los Angeles late in the season, it was practically front-page news. The Lakers had enough requests for tickets to the game to sell out the building many times over! Magic was back, and that meant the fun was back for fans and players alike.

In 1982, however, the lovable Magic turned into a villain. It was his early-season complaints about the Lakers' dull offense that had caused coach Paul Westhead to be fired. But his unselfish team play quickly helped him to earn back the respect of his fans. Johnson became only the third player in NBA history to collect more than 700 assists and 700 rebounds in the same year.

With Magic showing the way, Los Angeles breezed through the play-offs and into the 1982 championship series against the 76ers. There Johnson struck a blow for the unsung skills of basketball. Despite ranking only fourth on his team in scoring in the series, his great passing, rebounding, and defenses against Julius Erving were praised as the key factors

In the 1982 NBA title series, the 76ers found there was no way to stop Magic. Although both Bobby Jones and Andrew Toney harass the fallen Johnson, he still hits Jamaal Wilkes with a perfect pass.

in the Lakers' easy triumph over Philadelphia. At an age when most players were just learning how the pro game was played, Magic Johnson was tucking away his second championship Most Valuable Player Award.

2
Nate "Tiny" Archibald

The nickname "Tiny" did not come to Nate Archibald because he was short. His father was a fairly big man who was called "Big Tiny" for fun, so his oldest son was called "Little Tiny." But when watching Archibald play with the giants of pro basketball, it is obvious that the name fits him. The 6-foot, 1-inch Archibald weighs barely 160 pounds and looks like a mosquito buzzing among the other players.

Sometimes it is hard to believe that Tiny has survived so many years of bumps and bruises against such large people. But he has, just as he survived a childhood in one of the worst slums in New York, the south Bronx, where he was born in 1948. While he was growing up, his family squeezed nine people into a two-bedroom apartment.

While at Kansas City, Tiny drove the big guys dizzy and led the NBA in both scoring and assists.

Nate's father left the family when the boy was 12 years old. Being the oldest child, it was up to Nate to take over some of the role of father. The added pressure, plus an environment of crime and drugs, took its toll on the youngster. Archibald became a short-tempered, stubborn fellow who drifted along without much concern for his schoolwork. Later he gave his basketball coach, Floyd Lane, credit for straightening him out and helping him to work for some worthwhile goals. Then Nate settled down in school and played basketball so well that he was named to the All-City team in his senior year.

A college education had been totally out of the picture only a few years earlier, but Nate was ready to take that step in 1966. First he attended Arizona Western Community College to work on his grades so that he could attend a larger school. He found the hot Southwest to his liking and went on to enroll at the University of Texas at El Paso. The speedy guard earned the respect of the Cincinnati Royals (later the Kansas City Kings), and in 1970 they drafted him in the second round.

Archibald quickly found that he could use his eel-like moves to slip through the pros as easily as he had done in the college ranks. No matter how well he was guarded or how small the opening,

Tiny could squirt through and charge toward the basket. He drove deep inside the defense, throwing it into confusion. This usually left either him or one of his teammates in the open. Since the Royals were not blessed with great scorers, Archibald took the ball to the hoop more often than most ball-handling guards. After scoring 16 points per game his rookie year, he improved to 28 the next.

In 1972-73 when the team moved to Kansas City-Omaha, the slippery guard left defenses spinning. He dominated the Kansas City offense so completely that it sometimes seemed he was taking on the other team all by himself. Archibald led the league in scoring with 34 and assists with 11.4 per game, the first time anyone had led the league in both categories. But despite the huge load Tiny was carrying, the Kings remained just an average team.

Tiny, meanwhile, returned home in the off-season and was horrified by what he saw. He found some of his younger brothers and sisters involved with drugs and in trouble with the law. Determined to do something to help, Archibald set up educational services and counseling programs in the community and returned every summer to lend a hand.

Archibald finally seemed to be heading for a winner when he was traded to the New York Nets.

Nate "Tiny" Archibald

But the Nets, who had been champions of the American Basketball Association before moving to the NBA, were running short of cash. They dismantled their team and traded away stars such as Julius Erving for money. Tiny hurt his foot that year and played in less than half of the Nets' games, and the team stumbled to the bottom of the standings.

The Buffalo Braves landed Tiny in a trade the next year, but he tore his Achilles' tendon in preseason play. Archibald sat out the entire year and never put in an appearance in a Buffalo uniform.

The next season, the Boston Celtics took a chance that the veteran still had a few moves left in him. It seemed a poor risk because Archibald reported in overweight and in poor spirits from a year and a half of inactivity. The season was a nightmare as Tiny heard complaints that the most work he did as a Celtic was to cash his huge paychecks.

When Tiny returned home after the 1978-79 season, he felt so discouraged that he did not think he could be of much help to the neighborhood kids. So this time, the kids turned the tables on Tiny. They rallied around him, encouraging him to stay with basketball and to work hard. They even offered him advice on how to improve his game. Tiny was so impressed by this display of interest that he was determined not to let them down. He rejoined the Celtics the next year, ready to take on his usual role of ballhandler. By this time, he was also willing to back away from scoring duties. There were plenty of players capable of getting points, including rookie Larry Bird, if someone could set them up for shots.

Early in the season, both Archibald and the Celtics woke up from their sluggish season of the year before. Tiny ran the fast break, dodged through traffic, wove into the middle, and drove defenses toward him. Then at the last instant, he would pass

After a sluggish start with the Celtics, Archibald picked up the pace.

off or pull up and toss in a soft jumper. He finished second in the league in assists with 8.4 per game, but, more importantly, the Celtics were winning again.

In Boston's 1981 championship win over the Houston Rockets, Tiny showed what playmaking was all about. Here he passes off to an unguarded man after drawing three Rocket defenders to him.

The following year was even better. With Tiny handing out seven assists per game and adding 13.8 points, Boston tied the 76ers for the best record in the league. After coming from behind to edge Philadelphia in the Eastern Conference finals, they faced the Houston Rockets in the championship series. Boston led the series, three games to two, going into game six in Houston.

Even though he was bothered by a sore leg, Tiny suited up and played a typical game. He made Houston earn every point they got and only turned the ball over twice to the clawing Rocket defense. On offense, he passed out scoring chances generously, dealing out 12 assists as the Celtics won the title with a 102-91 victory. With Tiny Archibald coming back home with his first championship, both he and the neighborhood kids could take pride in being winners.

In nine years as an NBA starter, Kevin Porter dished off more than 5,000 assists.

28

3
Kevin Porter

When it comes to excellence in providing assistance for other people, several names spring to mind. There is the Red Cross, the Boy Scouts, and Kevin Porter. Porter makes the list because of his unmatched record of assists in the NBA.

The category of assists was set up in an effort to recognize the value and skill of the playmakers. Any player who throws the ball to a man who is in position to take a high-percentage shot gets credit for an assist, providing the shot is successful. If the scorer has to make any move to break free for a shot after catching the pass, no assist is awarded. Pro coaches consider six assists per game to be a generous contribution from a player. Porter, however, has topped 20 assists on more than a dozen occasions.

In fact, 6 of the top 11 assist performances in the NBA have come from this little guard.

Kevin was born in Chicago, Illinois, in 1950. He grew up near DuSable High School, one of the most famous basketball schools in the state. Jim Brown had earned widespread respect there for his well-coached teams. When Porter joined the DuSable Panthers, he learned the value of setting high goals and working to reach them. For the first time in his life, he made up his mind to go on to college. When he graduated in 1968, he proudly accepted an offer to enroll at St. Francis College in Pennsylvania as an education major.

Kevin's college play gave few clues as to the role he would take as a pro. There he used his speed to break free from opponents and to get shots for himself rather than set up his teammates. In his three years as a starter, Kevin averaged 23.6, 23, and 24.7 points per game.

Pro scouts, however, were not sold on Kevin as a prospect. At only 5 feet, 11 inches, Porter would be one of the smallest men in recent years to play pro basketball. Pros feared that opposing guards would have an easy time popping shots over his head. Because of his height, in 1972 he was not drafted by the Baltimore Bullets until the second round.

Kevin Porter

The Bullets (who later moved to Washington) soon found that their new guard had special playmaking qualities. While he would always have to struggle on defense, offense was a different story for Kevin. He could dribble downcourt faster than most players could run, and his fast starts and changes in direction made him a valuable man whenever the Bullets got into a fast-break match with the other team.

That first year, Porter earned a spot on the team and was used as a reserve. When he did play, he made sure the ball went to an open man. Although he played only 20 minutes a game in 1972-73, he still averaged 6½ assists per game.

Porter made a lot of Bullets happy during his next two years with the team. He improved his assist record to a league-leading 8 per game in 1974-75. But after that season, he was traded to the Detroit Pistons. There it took him awhile to adjust to his new teammates, and he failed to regain his position as the league's top assist man. Midway through the 1977-78 season, he found himself traded again, this time to the New Jersey Nets.

Playing for the woeful New Jersey franchise that season was more like hard labor than a game. But Porter made life more bearable for the losing Nets and their fans by passing out scoring chances. In February of 1978, Porter was especially generous. Throughout the game, he threaded passes through the Houston Rocket defense. Then he watched his grateful teammates cash in on the chances he had given them. Before the game was over, Porter was given credit for 29 assists, an NBA record! Considering that each assist resulted in 2 points, Kevin set up 58 easy points for his team. That performance helped him to win his second league assist title with a season average of 10.2.

Porter searches for a weakness in the Atlanta Hawks' defense.

The next season, Porter was back at Detroit. This stay with the Pistons was more successful than his first, and he enjoyed an incredible year. Kevin would pass the ball to his teammates as smoothly as if he were dealing cards. Although the Pistons were not the best of shooters, they scored often, courtesy of Porter. He earned a league record 1,099 assists for the year, giving him a 13.4 average. When added to his 15.4 points per game, this meant that Kevin accounted for over 42 points per game.

Houston's Mike Dunleavy tries to stop the Detroit Pistons' ace.

Still Detroit did not win very often. Desperate to somehow find a winning combination, they again traded Porter away. Kevin went to the Washington Bullets, where he received a disappointing welcome. The Bullet coach thought Porter did more harm than good in the lineup, and his defensive shortcomings and fast-paced style of play did not fit in with the Bullets' system. Kevin was left on the bench while the Bullets faded out of the play-off picture.

Back with the Bullets where he had started his career, Kevin flashes his old form.

Toward the end of the year, Porter was given another chance, and his return sparked the Bullets to new life. Players like Kevin Grevey and Greg Ballard praised him for helping them improve their play. The team rallied behind Porter and won a play-off spot for the 12th straight year.

There were still those, however, who thought that Porter's style of play was too wild for the Bullets. So in 1980 the Bullets drafted playmaker Wes Matthews with their number-one choice. Porter had to battle to keep the talented youngster from taking his job, but by the middle of the year the new playmaker had been sent to Atlanta. Kevin was still in charge in Washington, and he won the assist championship for the fourth time in his career with a 9.1 average.

Sidelined by an Achilles' tendon problem in 1981-82, Porter missed most of the season. Although he attempted to come back the following season, he was not able to make the Bullet team. Kevin's career in the pros appeared to be over.

For a retirement present, the NBA should give Kevin Porter free copies of the league record book. After all, he singlehandedly wrote most of the section on assists.

4
Quinn Buckner

In 1972 when colleges voted to allow freshmen to compete in varsity sports, there were some who thought the idea was silly. Putting scared kids just out of high school against seasoned college players was like throwing lambs to the wolves, they thought. But instead of getting chewed up, the first college freshmen to play under the new rule held their own in competition. The most shining example of freshman skill was Quinn Buckner of Indiana University. Buckner made the switch from high school to major college competition as easily as if he were moving from one comfortable chair to another.

Quinn was born in Phoenix, Illinois, in 1954. He was a typical all-around sports star whose major problem in athletics was choosing which sport to play. Quinn led his Thornridge-Dolton High School to two straight Illinois state basketball titles, and most observers claimed that his football ability was equally great.

Buckner saw no reason to choose between the two sports, even when he enrolled at Indiana University. In the autumn, he reported to the football team. With his quickness, he could cover the entire middle of the field from his safety position. And at 6 feet, 3 inches, and 205 pounds, he was strong enough to tackle hard. Indiana also let Buckner weave through defenders on punt and kick-off returns. The freshman so dominated his position that he was a starter from the first play of the season.

When football ended, Quinn traded in his shoulder pads for a basketball uniform and started at point guard as a freshman. He played the same two sports the next season when it appeared that football was his better sport. During his sophomore season, the hard-hitting football star had trouble hitting anything when it came to basketball. Quinn's shots bounced off the rim all season, and he made only 34 percent of his shots.

Rather than convince him to stick with football, however, the disastrous basketball season had the opposite effect. Quinn was determined to do well

At Indiana University, Buckner directed one of the greatest teams in college history. All five starters for the 1976 champs went on to play in the pros.

at basketball, and he followed his coach's advice about quitting football in order to spend more effort on the roundball sport.

The extra practice paid off immediately. In his junior season, 1974-75, the scattershot Buckner zeroed in on his target. In one game, Buckner sank 13 of 14 shots. His shooting improved so much that Buckner actually led Big Ten guards in shooting that year with 56 percent. Defenders no longer could ignore Quinn's shooting, and that made his passing even more effective. Buckner was given much of the credit for leading the Hoosiers to an undefeated regular season. His tough defensive work frustrated many a high-scoring team, forcing them from their usual patterns into a mad scramble.

The favored Hoosiers did not win the college title that year, but they only had a one-year wait to make up for it. In 1976 Quinn sparked one of the top college teams of all time, with future pros Scott May, Bobby Wilkerson, Tom Abernethy, and Kent Benson all in the lineup. They easily shut down all their rivals to win the crown over Michigan.

The season had barely ended when Quinn was asked to join the United States Olympic team. A cool-headed leader would be desperately needed in order for the team to compete against larger, rougher foes who were more experienced in the special Olympic rules. Although many college stars sat out the Olympics for fear of an injury that would wreck their pro chances, Quinn took up the challenge. His steady passing and defense helped to keep the team together as they gained experience in the early Olympic rounds. By the final game, they were a typical, smooth-running Buckner team. The match against Yugoslavia for the gold medal was no contest with the U.S.A. winning, 95-74.

Good leaders are hard to come by in basketball, and the Milwaukee Bucks jumped at the chance to snatch Quinn in the first round of the 1976 draft. As usual he did not let his young age keep him from taking control of the veteran team. His performances never made very interesting news in his first three years, however, as he averaged fewer than 10 points a game. But he averaged more than five assists and started every game for the Bucks. Defensively, Quinn still had the quickness to cut off guards smaller than he as well as the strength to outmuscle larger guards. He quickly became the Bucks' all-time leader in steals. In a 1977 game against the Indiana Pacers, he swiped nine passes. Year in and year out, Buckner's stingy defense earned him praise as an opponent whom even the high-scoring guards feared.

Quinn takes it to the hoop for the Bucks against the Kings.

Several seasons later, however, the burdens of being a playmaker again threw Quinn's shooting off for awhile. In 1980 opponents backed away from Buckner, daring him to shoot while they concentrated on guarding the other Bucks. But Quinn rose to the challenge, regained his accuracy, and again forced the defense to guard him closely. He even scored 40 points in a single game and in 1980-81 improved his scoring average to 13.3.

Still Quinn did not let his improved scoring make him greedy. He knew that Marques Johnson, Bob Lanier, Brian Winters, and the rest were paid to score, and Buckner was paid to see that they got the chance. The Bucks played confidently, knowing that they did not need to look around for someone to take charge. Buckner did his job well enough to help Milwaukee earn their second straight divisional title in 1980-81.

Buckner's value to the club was best shown by his absence in 1982. With Quinn benched by an injury, the powerful Bucks fizzled at the end of the year. The leaderless team did not even survive their first round of the play-offs.

Then before the 1982-83 season, Buck fans and players alike were shocked by the announcement that Quinn had been traded to the Boston Celtics

The big trade of 1982 sent Buckner to Boston in exchange for the Celtics' great center, Dave Cowens.

Quinn Buckner

for Dave Cowens. Many thought that was a steep price to pay for the ex-Celtic star who had not played for several seasons. Boston, however, could not have been more pleased. They felt certain that with Buckner in control, the Celtics would remain one of the league's classiest teams for years to come.

As the Chicago Bulls find out, Johnny Davis is a hard man to pin down.

5
Johnny Davis

If it is played properly, a full-court press can make some of the most poised ball handlers hit the panic button. In this defense, the plan is to double-team the man with the ball deep in his own end of the court. The defenders try to give the ball handler so little room to breathe that he throws a desperate pass that can be intercepted. Although the method is not found in any coaching books, there does, however, seem to be one sure-fire way to beat a full-court press. Simply give the ball to Johnny Davis and see if there are any two men alive who can box him into a corner. So far Davis has found all full-court presses to be as confining as a run through a park!

The Johnny Davis story is a familiar tale of many

basketball stars from the inner cities. Born in Birmingham, Alabama, in 1955, Johnny moved with his family to Detroit at the age of two. There he lived in a rough housing project but managed to avoid getting into trouble. After taking up the sport of basketball, he sharpened his skills by playing against local talent and went on to average 31 points per game in high school.

Davis earned a scholarship to Dayton University in Ohio and moved into the starting lineup as a freshman on a senior-filled squad. The new kid blended in well with the veterans, and at the end of the season Dayton was invited to the National Collegiate Athletic Association (NCAA) post-season tournament. It was like being invited to an evening of punishment because Dayton was forced to play UCLA in the Western Regional. As usual, UCLA was unbeaten that year, and their swarming full-court press was working to perfection. They could destroy an opponents' confidence by ganging up on the backcourt players from the opening tip. If their opponents did happen to break through, they still had College Player of the Year, Bill Walton, waiting near the basket. The 6-foot, 11-inch center was so good at stopping the fastbreak by himself that other UCLA players could afford to take chances.

The freshman Davis, however, apparently had not heard how overwhelming the UCLA press was supposed to be. He darted upcourt past defenders as if they were gates on a slalom ski run. Even the towering presence of Walton did not discourage Johnny. On one play, he kept running straight at Walton and laid the ball in the hoop over his head. With this kind of performance from their playmaking guard, Dayton gave undefeated UCLA its closest game of the year.

After two more years at Dayton, Davis decided that, with his mother laid off of her job due to surgery, he should try to earn some money as a pro. Portland picked him up in the second round of the 1976 draft and used him as a reserve guard. Davis' greyhound speed convinced the Trailblazers to use him on special occasions as a fast-break leader and for breaking through a tough defensive press. Johnny also showed skill at finding open lanes through which to get the ball to the big men under the basket.

For most of the season, Johnny saw little action and averaged only 18 minutes per 48-minute game. And when Portland was driving for a top play-off spot at the end of the season, Davis played even less. Team officials admitted that Johnny's future in

Portland star Bill Walton pushed for more playing time for Davis, which helped the Blazers win the 1977 title.

the pros seemed to be limited to spot duty rather than as a leader. But Davis did not complain and quietly did his job when he got the chance. He had learned early in his career that a team needed players willing to accept limited roles in order to be successful.

Bill Walton, now Johnny's teammate at Portland,

led the way as the Trailblazers swept into the play-offs with a fine record. There they found a tough play-off opponent in the Denver Nuggets, the best of the ABA teams that had joined the league that year. Walton, who perhaps still remembered that game against Dayton back in college, pushed to get Johnny Davis into the lineup. The Trailblazer coach agreed to try putting him into the sixth game of the close series to see if he could beat the Nuggets in a running game.

As Davis led his team to a 24-10 lead, the surprised Nuggets were left standing in their tracks. After a quick time-out, Denver tried to get back in the game by going to their full-court press. Davis treated their press as he had treated all others, and before long the score had widened to 36-16. Davis finished the game with 24 points and 4 steals and helped Portland win, 108-92, and advance to the final round of the 1977 championship. Their opponent, the Philadelphia 76ers, posed a problem with the quick Henry Bibby at guard. Portland called on Davis to stop Bibby, and he did his job well. The Trailblazers swept the final four games of the series to win the title, four games to two.

Johnny was rewarded with a more active role the following year. He was a key man in the perfect blend of teamwork and passing that helped the Trailblazers outclass the rest of the league. But after an overpowering 58-24 record in the regular season, Portland's big men went out with injuries, and the team failed to defend its title.

By this time, Portland was fond of Davis, but they were even more fond of University of Minnesota center Mychal Thompson. Before the 1978 draft, Portland traded Davis to the Indiana Pacers for the chance to get Thompson in the college draft. Davis found very little to work with on the Pacers, and, as a result, he was torn between trying to be the playmaker and trying to do the scoring. It was a difficult time in his career as Indiana suffered through a couple of terrible seasons.

Johnny's patience with his new team paid off in 1980-81. He contributed 14.4 points and just over six assists per game as his team began winning. That season, the lowly Pacers surprised everyone by gaining their first play-off berth since joining the league in 1976. The next season, Davis seemed to be a one-man team at times. With a scoring average of 17 per game, he achieved the rare honor of leading his team in scoring while directing the offense. Johnny Davis at guard would seem to provide the key to many more play-off berths in the future.

Davis, the top man for the Indiana Pacers, doesn't seem too worried about the Washington Bullets' defense.

When given a second chance in his basketball career, John Lucas, shown here going against the Celtics, tried to get his act together.

6
John Lucas

When John Lucas steps onto the court in front of screaming fans and fires a shot that drops into the netting, is he likely to be pleased or displeased with himself? It all depends on the season. John Lucas, the pro basketball player, would be satisfied with his two points. When he switches his identity to John Lucas, pro tennis player, he does not like to see his shots go into the net.

Lucas is one of the few athletes in modern times with so much talent that he has played two sports professionally in the same year. (Another was Dave DeBusschere who played with the Chicago White Sox and the Detroit Pistons in 1962-63.) Juggling those two careers has been quite a load for John, but it was nothing compared to the load he carried during the 1980-81 season. That was a time when both the career and life of one of the NBA's brightest stars was near destruction.

John was born in 1953 and grew up in Durham, North Carolina, where his parents were both school principals. When it came to sports, John had a magic touch. He first picked up a tennis racquet when he was in the fifth grade. One month later, he won a city tournament. By the time he reached high school, he was nearly unbeatable in tennis and swept through 92 wins in a row. His high school football coach sized up Lucas as the best passer at the school, but he did not offer him a spot on the team. He was aware of John's amazing skill at other sports and did not want Lucas to risk a football injury.

Regardless of how well he did in other sports, basketball was number one with Lucas. He took advantage of his connections in high places, begging the keys to the school gymnasium whenever he could. After winning recognition as a high school All-American in basketball, John had to sift through a mound of scholarship offers from colleges. Over 350 schools wanted him to play basketball for them, and another 50 offered scholarships in tennis.

Lucas liked what he saw of the University of Maryland, especially since the coaches would allow him to play both basketball and tennis. The school, however, had to pass one important test. John's family had agreed that he would attend a school that was no more than a one-hour plane ride from their home. Lucas clocked the flight to Maryland. When the plane landed in 48 minutes, he enrolled.

Along with Quinn Buckner, John entered college in 1972 with the first freshman class that was allowed to play varsity sports. Lucas erased all doubts about whether or not he belonged with the older fellows when he made 9 of 10 shots in his first game. He was a natural leader and passer and was so quick that he did not even need a jump shot in college. John was one of the rare top-level players who still used the old-fashioned set shot.

John's quickness worked in tennis as well as in basketball, and he won the Atlantic Coast Conference singles title as a sophomore. Even though he only played the sport when he could squeeze it into his basketball schedule, John became the best tennis player in Maryland history. Pro teams in both of John's sports tried to get him to leave school and play for them. But John had been a principal's son long enough to know the value of education, and he stayed in school the full four years.

Upon graduating in 1976, Lucas finally had to make a choice as to which career he would pursue.

The Houston Rockets' stock rose when Lucas came to take control of the offense.

He still had not made up his mind when he received news from the Houston Rockets basketball club that made his decision for him. The Rockets made him the first player chosen in the draft that year, and John realized that, unless the scouts had blundered, he must have great potential in the sport.

The Rockets had never enjoyed a winning season before John's arrival. But with Lucas taking over the playmaking post, guards like Calvin Murphy and Mike Newlin were free to concentrate on shooting. The arrangement worked well enough to get the Rockets into the win column with a 49-33 record.

In his second season, John was one of the few Rocket players to stay healthy. While his teammates limped off with injuries, John kept playing hard. He averaged 12.4 points and finished second in the league in assists with a 9.4 average. But the Rockets missed the play-offs, giving Lucas enough time to play tennis for the New Orleans Nets.

With Lucas handling the ball, Murphy, Newlin, and Rudy Tomjanovich doing the shooting, and awesome rebounder Moses Malone back from injuries to play center, the Rockets expected big things in 1978. Things looked even brighter when they signed aging superstar Rick Barry to a contract. But their hopes were dashed when the league ordered Houston

59

John Lucas

to send Lucas to the Golden State Warriors as payment for signing Barry. That was a steep price to pay, even for someone with Barry's reputation.

It was hardly John's idea of a good break, either. Golden State had gone into a sharp decline since winning the NBA title in 1974-75. When John joined them, they were plunging to the bottom of the standings. The 6-foot, 3-inch Lucas rallied his teammates as best he could, averaging 8.5 assists and 14 points over the next two years.

In 1980-81 Golden State finally made some moves

to strengthen the club when they traded for two expert marksmen, Lloyd Free and Bernard King. After using draft choices to add center Joe Barry Carroll and rebounding forward Larry Smith, the Warriors seemed to have the ingredients of a winner. With Lucas playing his usual steady game, the Warriors started strongly. But it soon became obvious that something was wrong with Lucas. John had been a model player all his career, never missing practice. He had been the kind of friendly, eager-to-please athlete who was popular with everyone from players to writers to fans.

Suddenly his mood changed. John skipped six games and twice as many practices and was finally suspended from the team. People whispered that drugs were destroying his career. Unfortunately, the rumors about drugs turned out to be true.

One disaster after another rocked John's life that season. He had been very close to his grandmother and his high school coach, and both had died during the year. John also had trouble adjusting to his new guardmate, Free, who was a far more spectacular player than any of his previous teammates. All of this made Lucas seem a very bad risk to the Warriors, and they added to John's worries by passing up a chance to renew his contract.

During the off-season, John finally got help for his depression, and admitted to having a cocaine problem. With proper treatment, he was able to overcome his problems, and he waited for a chance to prove to some NBA team that he could still do the job.

The Washington Bullets took a chance on Lucas during the 1981-82 season. There he shared time with rookie Frank Johnson and began to regain his old form. The Bullets were hoping that John would complete his comeback and become the player he had been when he first entered the league. A recharged John Lucas could ease the minds of a good many Bullet players who could use the services of one of basketball's finest athletes.

7
Norm Nixon

Ron Nixon had come back home to Georgia from a stint in the armed forces. He decided to go out with some friends to relax and watch some of the local high school teams play football. It did not take long for the game to produce an exciting play worth the price of admission. The kickoff floated toward the goal to where a small player was standing. He caught the ball, raced up the middle of the field, and bolted to the outside. None of the tacklers could get a grip on him, and the runner broke loose for a touchdown.

Like many of the spectators at the game, Ron was amazed by the long run. "Who is that player?" he wanted to know. The answer he received was even more startling than the run. It turned out that the mystery back was Ron's own little brother, Norm!

Norm Nixon gets past rival backcourt star Johnny Davis (16) and scores two against the Pacers.

Norm Nixon has been taking people by surprise throughout his sports career. Many fans have settled into their seats to enjoy a game and been quickly fascinated by an unknown player running his foes ragged. "Who is that player?" Nixon has caused that question to be asked wherever he has played.

Norm, born in 1955, was the youngest child of the Nixon family in Macon, Georgia. His mother developed a muscle condition that weakened her, and Norm had to help out around the house quite a bit. He grew to be an exceptionally neat person, always wanting to see things in their place.

Norm was the one who seemed out of place, however, when it came to sports like football or basketball. During his younger years, he was smaller than most kids. But he quickly showed that he had the skill and drive to fit in on any team. He made All-State in track, basketball, and football, and was a top student, a trumpet player, and president of his high school class.

Norm formed good basic basketball habits with some unusual help from his basketball coach. To increase his ball-handling skills, Nixon was forced to go through such drills as dribbling while wearing gloves. But despite his all-around ability, Norm did not attract the interest of many college coaches.

One person who did catch the coaches' eyes, however, was a Georgia high school player named Wayne "Tree" Rollins (who later played pro ball with the Atlanta Hawks). Rollins, a 7-foot center, lured a crowd of college scouts to the Georgia state high school tournament in 1973. During one game while the scouts were watching Rollins, they could not help but notice a 6-foot, 2-inch guard who was leading the other team to a fine effort. Nixon and his teammates stormed to an easy win over the dominating center. Duquesne University of Pittsburgh was impressed enough to forget about Rollins and ask the familiar "Who is that player?" They found out and convinced Norm to attend their school.

Norm's first college scrimmage, however, was enough to send him running for cover. The play was so much rougher than anything he had ever known that he wondered if he belonged in college ball. But he regained his confidence fast enough to crack the starting lineup during that freshman year. The likeable math major went on to play four years, breaking the school record for assists and averaging over 20 points per game his final two seasons. His popularity did not spread far from the Pittsburgh campus, however, and Norm was not even invited to try out for the 1976 Olympic team.

Nixon proved he could take the bumps and shoves of college basketball and went on to star for Duquesne.

One of the coaches who did take a long look at Norm was a football coach, Chuck Noll of the Pittsburgh Steelers. He liked Nixon's quickness and coordination and thought he could make a good defensive back. But after watching him play basketball, Noll realized that Norm was already well on his way to a successful basketball career.

Proving there was room for two leaders on the court, Nixon (here driving on the San Diego Clippers) and Magic Johnson became the first pair of teammates to collect more than 600 assists each.

The Los Angeles Lakers chose Nixon at the end of the first round in the 1977 draft. Both the Lakers and their fans began asking the old question, but this time there was no way that fame would escape Norm. He broke into the starting lineup and showed such a flair as a playmaker that fans were reminded of the great Laker, Jerry West. He refused to be overwhelmed by the fact that he was playing with a basketball legend, Kareem Abdul-Jabbar, and played his usual, intelligent game. Besides controlling the fastbreak and whipping passes to Jabbar in the middle, Norm proved himself to be a smart shooter. He worked hard to get good shots and finished the year with a .497 shooting percentage, the best ever for a rookie guard in the league. Norm was recognized as an All-Rookie guard, passing over the more highly ranked backcourtmen who had been drafted ahead of him.

The next year, Nixon improved his scoring from 13.7 to 17.1 points a game and finished third in the NBA in assists with a 9.0 average. The statistics, however, did not stop the Lakers from drafting college basketball's passing wizard, Magic Johnson, the following year. It was a puzzling situation with two playmakers in the lineup at the same time. Nixon found himself in the familiar spot of drifting into the background while his guardmate was flooded with publicity.

As usual, Nixon fought back with his on-court performance. Instead of losing out to the new guard, he joined forces with him, and soon the Laker backcourt was considered the best in the league. In 1979-80 both players ranked in the top 10 in assists, with Nixon having the slight edge. Norm also took advantage of Johnson's passing to boost his own scoring average to 17.6.

Norm Nixon

The Lakers won their division that year and swept into the finals against Philadelphia. Though players like Abdul-Jabbar and Johnson piled up more impressive statistics, Norm played his usual consistent game. He averaged 15½ points per contest to help Los Angeles win the series, four games to two.

The next year, the burden was back on Nixon as Johnson went out for most of the year with an injury. Norm met the challenge by increasing his assists to 8.8 a game, second only to Kevin Porter.

Upon Magic's return to the lineup late in the year, Nixon moved back to sharing the ball-handling duties. While most teams searched for a top floor leader to direct their offenses, the Lakers were enjoying the luxury of starting *two* playmakers! They cashed in on more easy scoring opportunities than any other team in the league, as both Nixon and Magic Johnson ranked in the top *five* in the NBA in assists. Nixon's skill allowed Magic to concentrate more on rebounding in the 1982 play-offs, and the result was an easy NBA title for Los Angeles.

With his performance, Norm Nixon had proven that he could match up well with anyone as a ball-handling magician. He had finally made a name for himself and was recognized for the fine player that he was.

Hard work helped Phil Ford climb to the top of the basketball world.

8
Phil Ford

Even as a small boy, Phil Ford believed that life was meant to be lived on a basketball court. Playing with friends in Rocky Mount, North Carolina, where he was born in 1956, Phil wanted to keep at the game long after everyone else was ready to go home. Then when he could no longer convince others to continue, he resorted to more drastic means. Phil would bring cookies to the basketball court and feed his friends in exchange for more playing time.

Ford was so hooked on the game that he found it entering into all parts of his life. Although his parents, who were teachers, had seen many methods of preparing for tests, they must have thought their son's approach quite unusual. When Phil felt pressure from studying for exams, he would go out and shoot baskets to get himself relaxed. During one summer, he must have been seeing basketballs in his sleep as he spent up to 12 hours a day working at the game.

Having practiced as many hours as a veteran pro player, Ford moved far ahead of his classmates in the sport. Though the 6-foot, 2-inch guard had no height advantage on his foes in high school, he completely outplayed them. He once scored 48 points in a single half! Phil was not really tested as a player until he went to the University of North Carolina. There he became an instant star in one of the toughest basketball conferences in the country, the Atlantic Coast Conference.

Ford was one of those rare players who could combine playmaking with scoring so well that he was in complete charge of the offense. Although his main task was to set up teammates for scores, Phil could outshoot most of his teammates from anywhere on the floor. His speed and intelligent play always kept him a step ahead of the opposition. This made him the perfect guard to run North Carolina's "four-corners" offense. Whenever his team built up a lead late in the game, they would go into a semi-stall, with one player in each corner of the offensive court. This spread-out formation gave Ford plenty of room in which to run. Phil would whirl around the center of the court, dribbling and firing passes to the cornermen, with the defense in frantic pursuit. Few teams could match North Carolina at this game of keep-away, and once Ford and his gang had a lead, they rarely lost it.

In 1976 Phil was one of the younger players to make the United States Olympic basketball squad. Though older, more experienced players such as Quinn Buckner and John Lucas were also on hand, Ford made himself noticed. No one in Montreal could match his incredible speed as he buzzed up and down the court. Ford collected 54 assists in six games to do his share in bringing the gold medal to the U.S.A. Once that was accomplished, he returned to college where he won the 1978 College Player of the Year Award from *The Sporting News*.

Word got out that year that the Kansas City Kings planned to use their number-one draft choice to select Phil. While honored at the thought of being the second man chosen in the entire draft, Ford dreaded going to Kansas City. He had seen the Kings and their "every-man-for-himself" offense. Sometimes they seemed to cling to the ball as if they would never see it again if they threw it to someone else. Ford announced that he did not care to be a part of this style of play, and he warned the Kings not to draft him.

Ford has lured Phoenix Suns' center, Alvin Adams, away from the basket and looks for an open teammate under the hoop.

But Kansas City's coach, Cotton Fitzsimmons, believed that a player such as Ford could bring the last-place Kings to the top of their division. They drafted Ford and finally convinced him that the only reason the Kings played as they did was because they had no one like Ford to set up the offense.

Phil proved that the Kings' coach had been correct in his prediction. He pumped new life into a team that had failed to make the play-offs 11 of the past 12 years. An enthusiastic, emotional player who seemed to be on the go 22 hours a day, Ford sparked his teammates to give the same kind of effort. He instantly brought the team closer together with his constant chatter, teasing, and tricks before, during, and after practice. Top shooters like guard Otis Birdsong and forward Scott Wedman found shots easier to come by with Ford feeding passes to them. With Phil keeping the Kansas City offense running smoothly, the Kings regained their long-lost crown as champions of the Midwest Division.

The value of their new playmaker was obvious in a play-off series against the Phoenix Suns that year. Phil went into a slump and had a poor series. The Kings, who had no one else to take charge, went down to defeat, losing four of five games.

Ford and the Kings continued to make the play-

Phil bears down on defense against the Denver Nuggets.

offs the next two seasons. Ford added some scoring punch of his own to the offense, averaging 16.2 points in 1979-80 and 17.5 the following year. Meanwhile, he handed out scoring chances to his teammates at a faster rate than ever in 1980-81. His 8.8 assist average tied him for second place with Norm Nixon. Ford was bothered by injuries the latter part of the year, but he came back to spark his team to play-off success. They gained revenge on Phoenix, beating them to gain the Western Conference finals. There they were finally turned back by the Houston Rockets.

An eye injury stopped Phil's rise to the top in 1981-82. With his buddy, Birdsong, traded to New Jersey and his injuries hampering his performance, Ford and the Kings both flopped that season. Kansas City wasted no time in giving up on him and traded him to New Jersey.

Phil carried the Kings to success until an eye injury endangered his career.

Phil Ford

Ford's backcourt reunion with Birdsong was cut short, however, when the Milwaukee Bucks came calling. They had lost Quinn Buckner in a trade and were desperate for a playmaker. Early in the 1982 season, the Bucks dealt forward Mickey Johnson to New Jersey for Ford. Milwaukee had been thwarted in their title attempts for several years and hoped that Phil could regain his old form. They figured that Ford could be the final piece in their attempts to construct a championship team.

e a

acism

rom the v
cropper life

DATE DUE

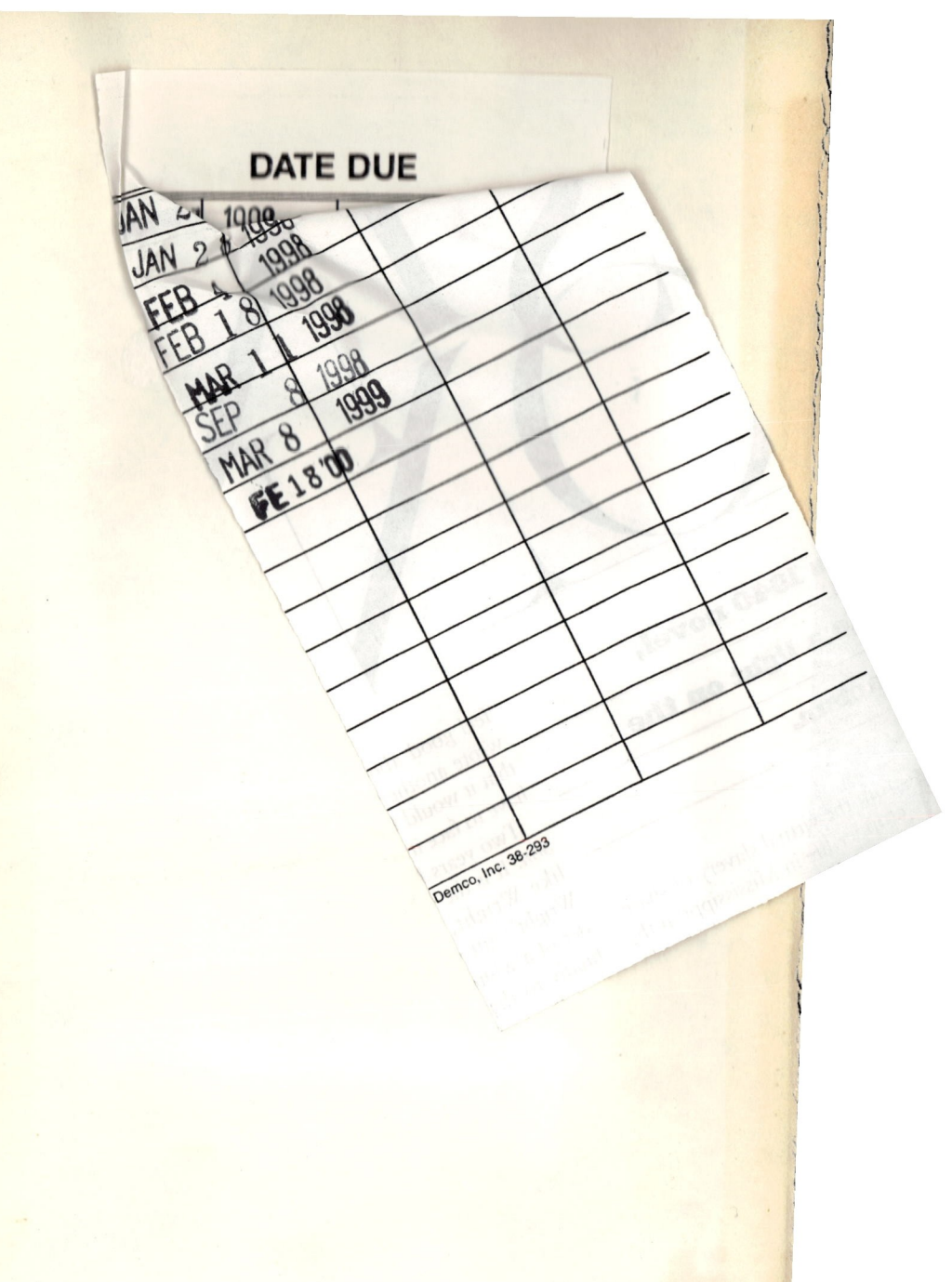

JAN 2 1998			
JAN 2 1998			
FEB 4 1998			
FEB 18 1998			
MAR 11 1998			
SEP 8 1999			
MAR 8			
FE 18 '00			

Demco, Inc. 38-293